BLISTS HILL
Victorian Town

Welcome to Blists Hill Victorian Town, part of the Ironbridge Gorge Museum Trust Limited. Founded in 1967, the Trust is a registered charity whose twin aims are education and heritage conservation. The Trust cares for 36 scheduled monuments and listed buildings within the beautiful Ironbridge Gorge World Heritage Site and operates 10 museums, which collectively tell the story of the birthplace of the Industrial Revolution. Our mission is to excel in researching, preserving and interpreting these sites for the widest audience and to enrich our visitors' experience with live demonstrations, hands-on activities and innovative educational programmes. We hope you have an enjoyable and inspirational visit.

CONTENTS

Numbers that appear in brackets within the text refer to the Exhibits' positions on the Plan

Introduction

Blists Hill Victorian Town has been developed over a number of years by the Ironbridge Gorge Museum Trust. Its purpose is to immerse visitors in the atmosphere of a small industrial town at a pivotal time in British history – the period between 1890 and 1910.

By 1890 the dramatic industrial, social and economic changes of the previous one hundred and fifty years had made Britain the most influential country in the world.

Standards of living for the majority of the population of the country had never been so good. Nutrition, health, sanitation, transport and communications had improved enormously. Everyone had access to state education for the first time in the nation's history which meant almost everyone under the age of twenty was numerate, could write and was able to read to improve their knowledge of the world, of science, of technology and of new discoveries. People read books for information and pleasure and turned to newspapers for the latest news, gossip and tales of terrible accidents and natural disasters. Between 1890 and 1910, the British public in every part of the country was well informed. They knew about other countries but were fiercely patriotic, believing in the British Empire and assured of their country's premier position in the world.

However, times were changing and Blists Hill Victorian Town is set in a period when Britain's economic, political and military power was being challenged and overtaken by other nations.

BLISTS HILL VICTORIAN TOWN
The Exhibits

'In the main town, there are a variety of jobs to be had.'

3

Jack Crabtree, Cycle Showroom
No.7a High Street
Fact file: part of building housing A.F. Blakemore & Son's grocery and provisions shop (see **4**)

2

Lloyd's Bank
No.5 High Street
Building status: copy
Original building: Lloyd's Bank, High Street, Broseley, Shropshire
Material: reclaimed local bricks
Date: c.1888
Contents: many items on loan from Lloyd's Bank
Date opened on site: 14th May 1987

'the grocer on
the High Street is looking
for another errand boy'

4

**A.F. Blakemore & Son,
Grocery and Provisions Shop**
No.7 High Street
Building status: copy (mirror image)
Original building: Owen's Grocer's
shop and warehouse, Market Street,
Oakengates, Telford
Material: specially made bricks
Date: c.1890
Contents: many items from Chester's
Salopian Stores, Westbury, Shropshire
Date opened on site: 14th July 2000

5

Bates & Hunt's Pharmacy and Chemist's Shop

No.9 High Street

Building status: based on original building

Original building: corner shop, Constitution Hill, Wellington, Telford

Material: reclaimed bricks

Date: c.1890

Contents: West Cliffe Pharmacy (latterly Pars & Co.), Poole Hill, Bournemouth

Date opened on site: 9th July 1984

'the very best working class students can secure some of the better jobs available if they apply themselves, in the local bank or chemist's for example'

TEETH
CAREFULLY
EXTRACTED

6

London & North Western Railway Goods Shed
High Street
Building status: based on original building
Original building: official railway company drawings and photographs of similar structures
Material: modern timber
Date: c.1880
Date opened on site: 23rd September 2003

7

W. Corbett & Co., Iron Merchants
No.1 Canal Street
Building status: based on original building
Original building: main facade of W. Corbett & Co, Iron Merchants, Church Street, Wellington, Telford (yellow brick coach entrance based on a number of local examples)
Material: steel frame, blocks and render
Date: c.1820 with mid-Victorian shop front
Contents: Museum collection
Date opened on site: 4th April 2009

McClures General Draper and Outfitters
No.3 Canal Street

Building status: based on original building

Original building: Stafford Place, Oakengates, Telford (façade of building and shop front)

Material: specially made engineering blue bricks to simulate those made and used in Telford in the 1860–80s; reclaimed slates

Date: c.1880

Contents: various

Date opened on site: 4th April 2009

'It's a pleasant shop to work in.'

9

Post Office and Stationers

No.5 Canal Street

Building status: invented

Original building: shop front copy of original on High Street, Shrewsbury

Material: specially made dark brown bricks to simulate those made and used in Telford in the mid to last half of the 19th century; reclaimed roof tiles

Date: *c.*1840

Contents: Victorian shop counters with display cabinets from shop in Oakengates, Telford

Date opened on site: 4th April 2009; Museum of the Post Office in the Community opened on the first floor in 2010

The Terrace
Nos.2–8 Canal Street
Building status: copy
Original building: Severn Terrace, New Road, Ironbridge, Telford
Material: specially made, Imperial proportioned yellow bricks to match those made and used in South Telford in the mid 19th century; reclaimed roofing tiles
Date: c.1840
Contents: Museum collection
Date opened on site: 4th April 2009

10

**Rowland Percy Smitheman
The Photographer's House**
No.7 Canal Street
Building status: based on original building
Original building: typical local examples, especially one on Wesley Road, Madeley Wood, Telford
Material: specially made orange/red bricks to simulate 18th and early 19th century low-fired examples made and used in south Telford; reclaimed handmade roofing tiles
Date: c.1790
Contents: Museum collection
Date opened on site: 4th April 2009

10

**Rowland Percy Smitheman
The Photographer's Studio**
No.7 Canal Street
Building status: based on original building
Original building: photographic evidence of similar Victorian structures in Telford
Material: modern timber
Date: c.1900
Contents: Museum collection
Date opened on site: 4th April 2009

11

Annie Pritchard's Confectionery and Sweet Shop

No.6 and 8 Canal Street

Building status: copy
Original building: shop window – The Anchor, Court Street, Madeley, Telford (with details from *c*.1905 photograph of sweet shop on Madeley Hill, Telford)
Date: *c*.1860
Contents: Museum collection
Date opened on site: 4th April 2009

12

Terrace Wash House

behind the Terrace on Canal Street

Building status: based on original building
Original building: remains of the wash house behind Severn Terrace, New Road, Ironbridge, Telford
Material: specially made dark brown bricks to simulate those made and used in Telford in the mid to last half of the 19th century; reclaimed roofing tiles
Date: *c*.1840
Contents: Museum collection
Date opened on site: 4th April 2009

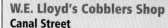

14

W.E. Lloyd's Cobblers Shop

Canal Street

Building status: rebuilt brick by brick
Original building: Oakengates, Telford (originally built as a weighbridge office before being occupied by W.E. Lloyd, cobbler, *c*.1920)
Material: original local brick; window and door
Date: *c*.1880
Contents: came with building
Date opened on site: 29th November 1978 (moved following a landslip on 9th February 1988; moved again and opened in present location 12th April 1990)

13

Fried Fish and Chipped Potato Shop

No.2 and 4 Canal Street

Building status: copy
Original building: shop front – High Street, Madeley, Telford
Date: *c*.1860
Contents: fish fryer – based on photograph of original made by Faulkner & Co., Hollins Road, Hollinwood, Oldham, shortly after the end of the First World War (photograph in Greater Manchester County Record Office collection, 2107-35)
Date opened on site: 4th April 2009

'The newly opened fish and chipped potato shop has certainly proved popular.'

15

New Inn Public House
No.11 High Street
Building status: copy
Original building: New Inn Public House, Green Lane, Walsall
Material: rendered blocks with original doors and windows from the above
Date: c.1880
Contents: came with building and from Museum collection
Date opened on site: 22nd June 1983

17

C. Jesse's Butcher's Shop
No.13 High Street
Building status: brick by brick
Original building: Waterloo Street, Ironbridge, Telford
Material: original local bricks, shop front and windows
Date: c.1850
Contents: butcher's shops in Oakengates, Dawley and Ironbridge, Telford
Date opened on site: 18th March 1980

16

Boys' Brigade Hut
High Street
Building status: invented
Material: modern timber
Date opened on site: 27th October 2009

'some still prefer to catch their meat illegally by poaching'

'The foundry can cast almost anything in iron and employs some good men, those making the wooden patterns are particularly talented.'

18

S. Corbett & Son's Foundry
between High Street and the canal
Building status: original building in situ
Original building: brick drying shed
Material: local bricks and roofing tiles
Date: c.1870
Contents: various sources including Bucklebury near Reading, Berkshire; Corbetts of Wellington, Telford; Hinksay Foundry, Dawley, Telford; and Northwich
Date opened on site: 21st June 1985

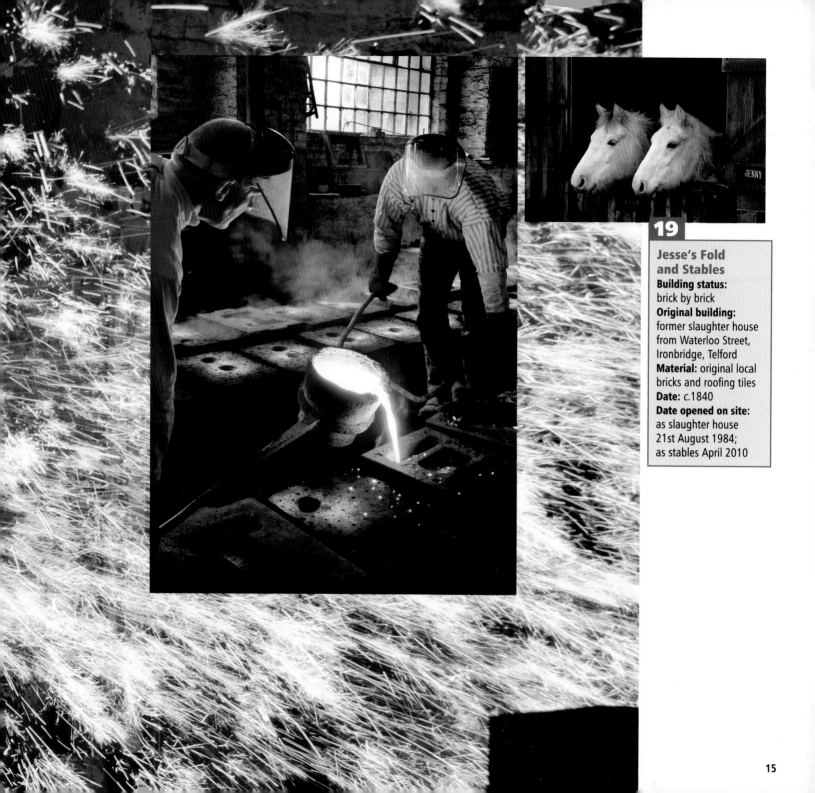

19

Jesse's Fold and Stables
Building status:
brick by brick
Original building:
former slaughter house
from Waterloo Street,
Ironbridge, Telford
Material: original local
bricks and roofing tiles
Date: c.1840
Date opened on site:
as slaughter house
21st August 1984;
as stables April 2010

'It is imperative to be able to spell correctly – and read back-to-front.'

20

John Edmunds Printer and Stationer's Shop
No.17 High Street

Building status: invented but incorporating an original shop front from a grocer's on Gower Street, St Georges, Telford

Material: reclaimed bricks

Date: c.1880

Contents: various sources including 19th-century equipment from Kington, Herefordshire

Date opened on site: 1973 (the first 'new' Victorian building on High Street, Blists Hill)

21 & 23

**B.A. Garbett, Plumber
and H. Topp, Tinsmith**

Canal Side

Building status: invented

Material: specially made dark
brown bricks to simulate those made
and used in Telford in the mid to last
half of the 19th century; reclaimed
roofing tiles; cast-iron windows from
Museum collection

Date: c.1880

Contents: tinsmithing and plumbing
equipment and stock of former Topp
family business, Bedworth,
Warwickshire

Date opened on site: 4th April 2009

22

T. Biddulph, Plasterer
Canal Side
Building status: invented
Material: modern timber
Date: c.1900
Contents: equipment and stock of former decorative plasterers; Thomas Biddulph, Burton-upon-Trent, Staffordshire
Date opened on site: 1980 (moved from site next to Sawmill following landslip on 9th February 1988; moved to present position next to the canal, enlarged and opened 4th April 2009)

24

Jack Crabtree Engineering Works (Machine Shop)
attached to the Foundry behind High Street
Building status: original building in situ
Original building: brick drying shed
Material: local bricks and roofing tiles
Date: c.1870
Contents: Museum collection
Date opened on site: 21st June 1985

25

R. Nevett, Mason and Builder's Yard
High Street
Building status: invented
Material: reclaimed bricks supporting original, local cast-iron roof trusses
Date: c.1880
Contents: J. Bysouth of the Worshipful Company of Stonemasons; and a Bristol stonemason
Date opened on site: 8th June 1991

26

Lee Dingle Bridge
(off) High Street
Building status: in situ remains (originally built for a plateway carrying coal between Meadow Pit, Madeley and Blists Hill)
Material: wrought iron supported on engineering brick piers
Date: 1872

'over the years it has brought up coal, ironstone and clay, but it now supplies clay to one of the nearby brick and tile works'

28

Lowe & Fletcher, Locksmith
(off) High Street
Building status: invented
Material: reclaimed bricks with cast-iron windows from Museum collection
Date: c.1890
Contents: Museum collection
Date opened on site: 11th October 1985

30

Trevithick Steam Locomotive
Canal Side

Status: replica of the world's first steam locomotive constructed in Coalbrookdale to the designs of Richard Trevithick (1771–1833)
Date: 1802/3
Fact file: replica built by apprentices at GKN Sankey, Telford at the end of the 1980s; ran briefly on a circle of track in Coalbrookdale and was eventually moved to Blists Hill in 2000

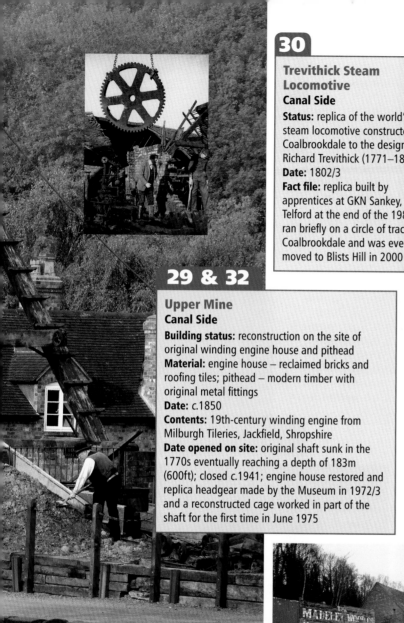

29 & 32

Upper Mine
Canal Side

Building status: reconstruction on the site of original winding engine house and pithead
Material: engine house – reclaimed bricks and roofing tiles; pithead – modern timber with original metal fittings
Date: c.1850
Contents: 19th-century winding engine from Milburgh Tileries, Jackfield, Shropshire
Date opened on site: original shaft sunk in the 1770s eventually reaching a depth of 183m (600ft); closed c.1941; engine house restored and replica headgear made by the Museum in 1972/3 and a reconstructed cage worked in part of the shaft for the first time in June 1975

31

Madeley Wood Brick & Tile Works
Canal Side

Building status: in situ remains
Original building: Madeley Wood Company Brick & Tile Works
Material: local bricks and roofing tiles
Date: 1870s
Date opened on site: (works abandoned after the Second World War); first cleared by the Museum in the 1970s then consolidated for public access in 1994

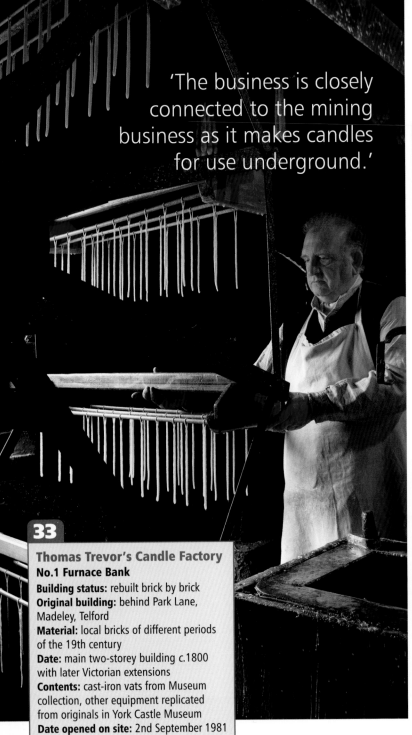

'The business is closely connected to the mining business as it makes candles for use underground.'

33

Thomas Trevor's Candle Factory
No.1 Furnace Bank
Building status: rebuilt brick by brick
Original building: behind Park Lane, Madeley, Telford
Material: local bricks of different periods of the 19th century
Date: main two-storey building c.1800 with later Victorian extensions
Contents: cast-iron vats from Museum collection, other equipment replicated from originals in York Castle Museum
Date opened on site: 2nd September 1981

34

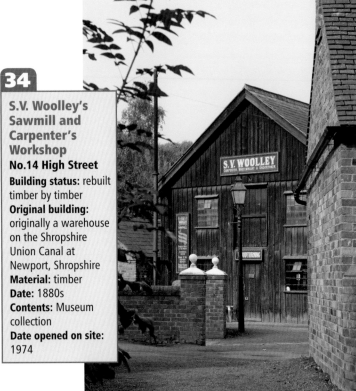

S.V. Woolley's Sawmill and Carpenter's Workshop
No.14 High Street
Building status: rebuilt timber by timber
Original building: originally a warehouse on the Shropshire Union Canal at Newport, Shropshire
Material: timber
Date: 1880s
Contents: Museum collection
Date opened on site: 1974

Pigs were not only a food source…

…their fat could be rendered down to produce tallow for candles

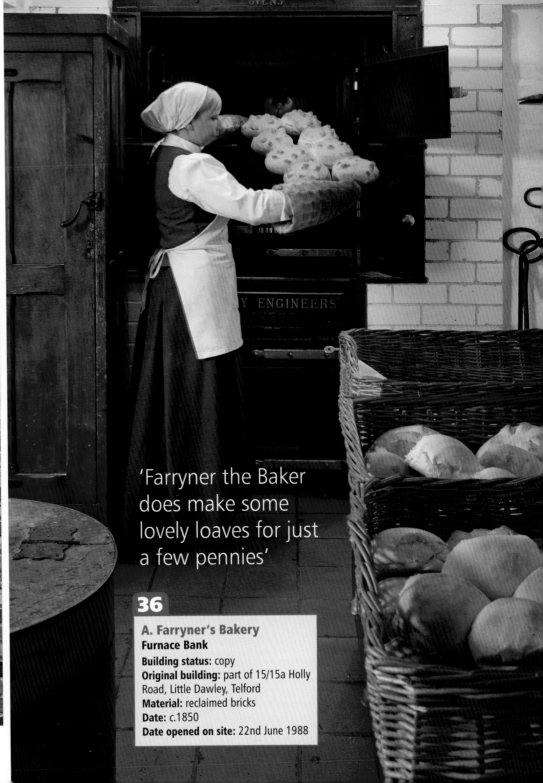

Thurmott, Saddler and Harness Maker
Furnace Bank
Building status: invented
Material: reclaimed local bricks and cast-iron windows from Museum collection
Date: c.1890
Contents: Thurmott family saddlers and harness makers of East Anglia who ceased to trade in 1972
Date opened on site: June 1993

'Farryner the Baker does make some lovely loaves for just a few pennies'

36

A. Farryner's Bakery
Furnace Bank
Building status: copy
Original building: part of 15/15a Holly Road, Little Dawley, Telford
Material: reclaimed bricks
Date: c.1850
Date opened on site: 22nd June 1988

37

Estate Office
Furnace Bank

Building status: timber by timber
Original building: part of the timber-framed structure of 15/15a Holly Road, Little Dawley, Telford; once The Crown Inn public house
Material: original timber – cruck and box framing; (bricks recovered proved unusable)
Date: 17th century
Contents: Museum collection
Date opened on site: 16th May 1991 (after recording and dismantling between 1983 and 1986)

38

Gospel Car
Canal Side

Status: originally built as a double-decker tramcar for Birmingham & Midland Tramways working in Wolverhampton; converted into a Sunday School for Bridgnorth Peoples' Hall Mission at Eardington, Shropshire in October 1928
Material: timber and tin
Date: 1904
Contents: Museum collection
Date opened on site: 1972

'The arrival of a doctor from Birmingham has lifted the spirits of the community. Everyone doffs their caps when the doctor walks by.'

39

Doctor's House and Surgery
No.2 Furnace Bank
Building status: rebuilt brick by brick
Original building: majority of one Duke of Sutherland's cottage built on Wellington Road (no.15), Donnington, Telford
Material: local brick
Date: 1862
Contents: Museum collection
Date opened on site: 22nd October 1986

40

G.R. Morton's Wrought Ironworks

Building status: main structural ironwork from central part of Woolwich Dockyard's anchor forge building designed by John Rennie (1761–1821) and acquired by the Museum in 1974

Material: cast-iron columns, wrought-iron ties, roof of tin sheets, (end walls of reclaimed brick)

Date: 1815

Contents: Walmsley's Atlas Forge, Bolton, Lancashire (acquired by the Museum in 1976 after works closed)

Date opened on site: officially opened 6th March 1987 by HRH The Prince of Wales (construction work had started in 1982)

'there's an impressive steam hammer that certainly makes the earth shake when it's working'

41

Madeley Wood Company Blast Furnaces

Building status: in situ remains
Original building: Madeley Wood Company Blists Hill Blast Furnaces
Material: local bricks
Date: base of first furnace, 1832; base of second and south engine house, 1840; base of third, 1844; north engine house c.1873
Contents: vertical blowing engine (c.1886) from the Lilleshall Company's Priorslee Ironworks, Telford (acquired by the Museum and fitted into the north engine house in 1971)
Date opened on site: furnaces blown out in 1912; all metal machinery and equipment scrapped by the 1920s; site first cleared by Museum in the 1970s then major consolidation carried out in 1994

42

Ironwork Offices

Building status: invented
Material: reclaimed bricks
Date: c.1880
Contents: Museum collection
Date opened on site: c.1987

43

Fairground
Lower Green

Fact file: 'Chairoplane Ride' based on c.1860 horse ride updated in the 1920s; 'swing boats' 1920s; Box Truck built by Savages, Kings Lynn, Norfolk in 1893; side stalls built by Marklands of Newton-le-Willows in the 1920s; coconut shie originally owned by the Smith family of Coventry.

Date opened on site: 1998

44

Blacksmith's Shop
Lower Green

Building status: invented

Material: reclaimed local bricks

Date: 1890s

Contents: Museum collection

Date opened on site: 1991 (the Museum had opened a blacksmith's workshop on High Street in 1984 but that was damaged beyond repair in the landslip of 9th February 1988)

The Forest Glen Refreshment Pavilion
Lower Green

Building status: reconstruction
Original building: part of the remains of the original Forest Glen, The Wrekin, Shropshire
Material: many original timbers
Date: 1889
Contents: modern 'heritage' furniture and lighting
Date opened on site: 24th May 1994

'When the fair pitches up next to the ironworks there's much fun to be had on the rides and swings.'

The Icebreaker
Fact file: when the Shropshire Canal froze, boats like this were rocked from side by side by a team of men to break up the surface ice; this example, named 'Middlewich', was acquired by the Museum from Chester in the 1970s and restored on a number of occasions.

Tub Boat
Fact file: made of wrought-iron sheets by the Lilleshall Company in the 18th century, this example carried about 5 tonnes of goods. Boats like this were designed specifically for use on the Shropshire Canal where they could be attached together and towed along in 'trains'; individually they would be floated into the cradles of the various canal inclined planes (such as The Hay Inclined Plane) so they could be moved between sections of canal at different heights. Until it was rescued by the Museum in the early 1970s this tub boat was being used as a cattle trough.

'almost everyone under the age of twenty was numerate, could write and was able to read'

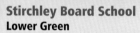

46

Stirchley Board School
Lower Green
Building status: rebuilt brick by brick
Original building: Stirchley Board School, Stirchley, Telford
Material: local brick
Date: 1881 (remained in use as a school until 1973)
Contents: Museum collection
Date opened on site: 26th June 1992

47

David & Sampson Blowing Engines
Lower Green

Fact file: from Lilleshall Co's Priorslee Ironworks where they were used to blow air into the blast furnaces. Used as standby engines between 1900 and 1952. Furnaces blown out 1959

Date: 1851 (made by Murdock, Aitken & Co, Glasgow)

Date opened on site: 1971 (sited next to what was at the time the entrance to Blists Hill)

48

The Spry
Lower Green

Fact file: based around remains of the original lower Severn Trow, 'Spry' was built by William Hurd, Chepstow. Until 1910 it transported limestone between the Chepstow quarries and Newport, Cardiff, Avonmouth, Sharpness, Bristol and Lydney. By 1932 all rigging had been removed so it could be towed as a barge and it was abandoned in the 1950s

Date: 1894

Date opened on site: arrived at Blists Hill 27th March 1983 from Diglis Basin, Worcester. Restoration completed in 1996. Sailed during 1996 and 1997 before being returned to Blists Hill in October 1997

Inclined Lift/railway
between Lower Green and canal
Building status: invented
Material: modern timber
Date opened on site: constructed on site during 2009

'Traditionally, mining and the iron trades have employed the most people who live in and around the town.'

51

Mine Railway and Mine Experience

Fact file: a battery-powered electric locomotive built by Alan Keef Ltd, and typical of the sort of equipment used in small mines after the First World War, runs on two foot gauge track into simulated underground workings where the experiences of local miners are brought to life.

Date opened on site: 2009

'damp squatter's cottage, thrown up in a matter of days and where children were always ill'

52

Squatter's Cottage
Building status: reconstruction
Original building: remains of a squatter's cottage, Burrough's Bank, Little Dawley, Telford
Material: stone and brick from original building
Date: between 1825 and 1841
Contents: Museum collection
Date opened on site: June 1979 (erected during 1978; adjoining pig sty and privy finished 1979)

53

Shelton Toll House

Building status: reconstruction
Original building: Holyhead Road toll house from Shelton, Shrewsbury, designed by Thomas Telford (1757–1834) and built by George Edgecombe of Ellesmere, Shropshire
Material: bricks, roofing slates, cills, lintels, doorsteps, windows, and doors from original building
Date: 1829
Contents: Museum collection; Holyhead Road wrought-iron toll gate salvaged from Blaenau Ffestiniog; milestone from Knockin Heath (removed during 1973 roadworks there)
Date opened on site: 1973 (first building rescued by the Museum and rebuilt on Blists Hill)

56

The Hay Inclined Plane

Fact file: in situ remains of 1793 incline with slightly later engine house, taken over by the London & North Western Railway in 1857; last used c.1894 and officially closed 1907

Date opened on site: clearance of docks at summit undertaken by volunteers in 1968/69; 1969 undergrowth removed from main incline by detachment of the Territorial Army Royal Engineers, who, in subsequent years, also re-graded the slope; basin at foot of incline first excavated in 1974; rails laid by volunteer working parties in early months of 1975

54

St Chad's Mission Church (Church of England)

Building status: original
Original building: Lodge Bank, close to Granville Colliery, Telford
Material: timber and corrugated metal sheet
Date: 1888
Contents: majority from original building augmented by font, pine lectern, brass cross, and alms dish from St Paul's Church, Aqueduct, Telford: pews, offertory plate, hymn and prayer books from Broseley Parochial Church Council
Date opened on site: re-consecrated on 28th June 1978 by the Bishop of Hereford (following re-erection in 1977)

'taking tub boats loaded with coal from the top of the canal at Blists Hill down to the riverside at Coalport'

'All aspects of life seem to have changed since Queen Victoria first came to the throne in 1837.'

A Small Town Story

Blists Hill is not a real town. It is a museum set in over 20 hectares (50 acres) of land where iron was once smelted (**41**), coal and clay were mined (**29** & **32**) and where bricks and roofing tiles were made (**31**). The remains of those industries can still be found on site, but in the same landscape a small industrial town has been created. A brief history of how and why it was done appears at the end of this guide.

Much pleasure can be had by wandering around the site, looking in the buildings, listening to the costumed demonstrators and getting involved with the various activities. But this part of the guide has been written in such a way as to allow you to see Blists Hill through the eyes of a Victorian and experience it as though you really were visiting a small industrial town over a century ago. What would you think of Blists Hill at the very end of Queen Victoria's reign? What would a small industrial town, somewhere west of Birmingham, nestling in the historic East Shropshire Coalfield, really be like?

Well, like any town anywhere in the country Blists Hill would have been shaped by its geography, how it communicated with its neighbours and the rest of the country and most importantly, what type of work was available for its residents. It's not an old market town with handsome buildings. There's no monumental town hall; no real town centre. There is only one really old building, a timber-framed structure now used as an estate office for the Earl of Craven (**37**). The main town is comparatively new; grown up, ad hoc, from the end of the 18th century around a few coal and clay pits and a canal. Most of the three or four thousand residents earn their living through hard, manual work, in the mines or local brick and tile works, in the foundry (**18**) or at the ironworks (**40** & **41**). Some of the lucky ones work in the small shops in the town. Blists Hill is a working class town where everyone has to work physically hard for almost all their adult lives.

On our visit, everyone's at work. No time for idling during the day or during the night; the men are involved with continuous industrial processes that take no account of the human body clock. Men, women and many children work long hours. They have to

because there is always the fear of being laid off if business is slack or of becoming unable to work through injury. Only the very largest firms provide medical treatment for accidents at work. There's no national health service and no state unemployment benefit. Trades unions now provide some support in hard times, but employers try and discourage workers from joining them. When the forges closed in 1886 at Horsehay, just ten miles from Blists Hill, people believed there was a real threat of starvation. Many residents of Blists Hill will walk long distances to work in neighbouring communities. Some families have felt compelled to move to other areas of the country or even to emigrate to Australia or Canada in order to make a better life for themselves.

Traditionally, mining and the iron trades have employed the most people who live in the town of Blists Hill. Close to the canal that runs through the settlement there is a small mine that has been working since the 1770s (**29** & **32**). Over the years it has brought up coal, ironstone and clay, but it now supplies mainly clay to one of the nearby brick and tile works. About 20 men work at the mine and they can walk all the way from Blists Hill to Coalport – underground, appearing next to the River Severn through what they call the 'Tar Tunnel'! Just outside Blists Hill is Shawfield pit – also mining clay – and then there is Hills Lane pit further along the canal towards Madeley where they still mine coal. Older residents of the town can remember when the Children's Employment Commissioner visited Hills Lane in 1842 and was unhappy that a four year old was at work underground there. That was, of course, an extreme case, but mining is dangerous. On 27th September 1864, 4 boys along with 5 men were killed in that Madeley pit. There are women employed in

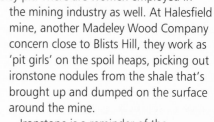

the mining industry as well. At Halesfield mine, another Madeley Wood Company concern close to Blists Hill, they work as 'pit girls' on the spoil heaps, picking out ironstone nodules from the shale that's brought up and dumped on the surface around the mine.

Ironstone is a reminder of the importance of the iron trades to this part of the country. Since the breakthroughs of the Darby family in Coalbrookdale in the 18th century, Shropshire has gained a national reputation for its iron work.

However, for some time now, since the 1870s in fact, job prospects in the local industry have not been good. Blast furnaces throughout the East Shropshire Coalfield have been 'blown out'. Although this term can be used to describe the temporary closure of a blast furnace for repair and rebuilding, its use recently in relation to local furnaces has been synonymous with permanent abandonment. Even the world famous Coalbrookdale Company no longer smelts iron, its last blast furnaces closing at Lightmoor and Dawley Castle in 1883. The three Blists Hill blast furnaces of the Madeley Wood Company (**41**) were 'blown out' recently and a local fortune teller predicts they will not work again after 1912. We'll have to wait and see!

Opposite those blast furnaces, G.R. Morton's ironworks is still in business making wrought iron (**40** & **42**). As ironworks go it's not that large and it's not particularly up-to-date either, but there's an impressive steam hammer that certainly makes the earth shake when it's working. It's used to hammer the impurities out of the spongy lumps of iron when they come out of the puddling furnaces. The sparks fly then! When the still red hot metal is threaded through those rattling iron rolls (or rollers to the uneducated!) and it snakes out across the black floor, thrown about by men as strong as horses who have to drink their weight in beer because they sweat so much, it is a real sight to behold. After all that physical effort you'll be surprised to learn that all that Morton's makes are simple wrought-iron bars that are sent to other places to be turned into chains and nails and other small metal industrial tools. Such a big place for such a basic product, so you can imagine how massive the Coalbrookdale Company's Horsehay ironworks must have been in 1843 to be able to roll the wrought-iron plates for what was at the time the largest ship in the world, the SS *Great Britain*. Business was better then.

Next to Morton's is a small blacksmith's shop (**44**) that uses wrought iron as its raw material. Every town needs a blacksmith, but Blists Hill also has an important foundry (**18**) that concentrates on making cast iron. At Corbett's Foundry they heat up scrap iron with coke and limestone until it's a liquid and can be poured into

sand moulds containing the pattern of the thing they want to make. The foundry can cast almost anything in iron and employs some good men, those making the wooden patterns are particularly talented. One apprentice attends art classes at the Coalbrookdale Literary and Scientific Institution and hopes to work in the art casting section of the prestigious Coalbrookdale Company Works one day. Attached to the foundry and run by Mr Crabtree is a well-equipped machine shop for precision work such as the planing and drilling of metal (**24**).

But if the Shropshire iron industry has been struggling over the last few years, then the local clay industries have been thriving and they now employ the most local people. They always need strong men, women and children in their works. In and around the town and particularly in Broseley, south of the River Severn, there are a number of quite large firms turning out millions of bricks and roofing tiles. They have earned a reputation for the high quality of their handmade products, but that reputation hides some

terrible working conditions. A visitor to the area in 1873 said those who worked in some of the 'brick yards', as they are called, were reduced to the level of beasts and their children he compared to savages. Fortunately, the industry is changing, and now machines are coming in that can press the clay almost automatically, replacing some of the worst repetitive and physically demanding work. These improvements should benefit the workers even though they have been introduced primarily to increase the profits for the owners.

Better jobs in the clay industry can be had almost within sight of Blists Hill, just south of the river, with the firms of Craven Dunnill and Maw & Co. who produce decorative floor and wall tiles for buildings all over the world. These firms, as well as the nearby Coalport China Works, employ a lot of skilled labour including young women. This makes a welcome alternative for girls who might otherwise have to go into service in the neighbouring large houses before marriage, or work long hours in some of the larger local shops. McClures Drapers and Outfitters shop (**8**) is one of the better class of establishment for a young woman to work for, retailing bolts of variously patterned fabrics as well as some ready-made garments. It's a pleasant shop to work in but obviously it is in a young woman's best interests to get married as soon as possible. Nevertheless, even after marriage with the husband as the main bread-winner, in many working class homes women have to find some form of paid work to be able to support a growing family until the children can begin to earn. Life can be particularly hard for the women of Blists Hill. If you have the business acumen of Annie Pritchard who, a few years ago, opened her own confectionery shop (**11**) in the house she rents on Canal Street, then at least you can be your own boss, with or without a husband.

In the main town, there are a variety of jobs to be had other than working with clay or iron. A.F. Blakemore & Son, the grocer on the High Street (**4**) is currently looking for another errand boy to work for the manager and his assistant, and alongside the two shop assistants, provisions hand and porter. Rumour has it Blakemore is soon to advertise for an apprentice as well. The sawmill run by S. Woolley (**34**) also has a small staff and R. Nevett the stonemason (**25**) has an apprentice stone cutter and will take people on when he has a building job. H. Topp the tinsmith (**23**), and particularly B.A. Garbett the plumber (**21**) are doing well at the moment. Amongst other things, Mr Garbett makes lead parts for the new 'water closets' being fitted into middle class homes. Not much demand in Blists Hill town itself, however, as outside 'earth closets' still suffice for the working classes. T. Biddulph the decorative plasterer (**22**) employs a number of men to carry out his jobs locally and it is one of the trades in which an artistic boy can exercise his talents if he is lucky to work there.

By comparison, little skill is needed in Thomas Trevor's candle-making business (**33**). It is a monotonous, smelly occupation that is certainly not the first choice of Blists Hill youngsters when they leave school and probably why Mr Trevor has to employ mainly family members. Too many rat problems for most people's liking.

The business is closely connected to the mining industry as it makes candles for use underground. Trevor isn't quite as busy as he used to be, the bigger and deeper pits now being obliged to use safety lamps rather than candles. Close to the candle factory, Mr Thurmott and his sons who make and repair horse harnesses (**35**) are busy most of the year simply because there are so many horses used in industry, farming and for local deliveries. Also in the leather trade, W.E. Lloyd (**14**) works alone in his tiny cobbler's shop watching the world go by, hearing all the gossip and adding to it when he gets an audience. No job opportunities there but he'll probably know where you can find work.

At the moment, the railway offers the best job prospects and security for a young man with ambitions. If he is fortunate enough to join the London & North Western Railway company that has a siding and goods warehouse in the town (**6**), then he will almost certainly have a job for life with guaranteed opportunities to better himself within that company if he's prepared to move around the country. The largest railway company in Britain can offer jobs anywhere on its network from Carlisle to London, or from Holyhead to Northampton.

So Blists Hill represents a true working-class town and is not much like those Victorian watercolours of idyllic rural life that are so popular at the moment. It's not a squalid place, mind you. It can get dirty at times, especially with all the smoke from the works. In summer the dust from the street blows everywhere and then when it rains things get quite muddy; but people have their pride. They are particularly fond of their small pleasure gardens (**27**) and there is always talk of a bandstand if the money can be raised. After all, the older residents of Blists Hill have seen enormous changes over the past few years.

It is not long ago, in 1881 in fact, that the new Board School (**46**) opened close to the ironworks. At first it was only compulsory for children between the ages of 5 and 10 years old to attend classes, but the limit has just been raised to 12. It has been very good for the community because if you can read, write and do some quite complicated arithmetic then you have a chance of securing some of the better jobs available, in the local bank (**2**)

or pharmacy (**5**), for example. It is also imperative to be able to spell correctly – and read back-to-front – if you are to work for John Edmunds the printer (**20**). Correcting type-setting mistakes is not only costly in time and labour, it can also be embarrassing if they are not spotted. Posters were once printed to advertise a 'grand tour in Wales' that came out as a 'grand rout in Wales'.

It is good that the children go to school. Childhood is still the most vulnerable period in a person's life. Like everywhere else in the country, they have large families in Blists Hill. Many children still die young from whooping cough, and scarlet fever. Fortunately, fresh water, piped to an increasing number of homes and businesses in Blists Hill through Corbett's cast iron (and Mr Garbett's lead) pipes has lifted the fear of another cholera outbreak like the one that killed so many in the 1830s. Typhoid is still a fresh memory for those who survived the epidemic of 1877, however. The arrival of a doctor from Birmingham has lifted the spirits of the community. He has just set up in practice in a cottage (**39**) overlooking Morton's Ironworks (**40**) with a surgery boasting all the latest equipment. As well as examinations, the doctor can also perform a number of minor operations. Everyone doffs their caps when he is seen in the town.

The doctor is a champion of improved housing. It has been known for a long time now that the type of houses people live in affects their health. It's good that there won't be any more built like that damp squatter's cottage (**52**) thrown up in a matter of days and where the children were always ill. It may look picturesque, but the doctor is right to campaign to have the occupants rehoused and the place knocked down.

He wants more buildings like the yellow brick terrace that was put up on Canal Street back in the 1840s. It certainly made the late 18th-century cottage immediately opposite, now occupied by Mr Smitheman the photographer (**10**), look very old-fashioned. Mr Smitheman probably doesn't worry about the age of his property, however, especially as he has just built a new wooden studio adjoining his house allowing him to expand his photographic portraiture business.

Improved standards of nutrition have been just as important for the health of Blists Hill residents as new housing. Many women still make their own bread at home, but Farryner the baker (**36**) does make some lovely loaves for just a few pennies. Most people grow their own vegetables as witnessed by the four tiny but well cared for gardens behind the terrace on Canal Street and the allotments opposite the candle factory (**33**). There is always the bonus of free food such as blackberries at certain times of the year, and some – to remain nameless individuals – still prefer to catch their meat illegally by poaching rather than patronise the butcher's shop on the High Street (**17**). The newly opened fried fish and chipped potato shop on Canal Street (**13**) has certainly proved popular, particularly with courting couples as there's a walk along the canal so close by. Some Blists Hill folk, however, have acquired a taste for more exotic fare such as those foreign bananas and tins of corned beef brought in by the London & North Western Railway and sold through the grocer's shop. At the beginning of Queen Victoria's reign, tinned produce was unheard of; now it's almost taken for granted.

It's quite a law-abiding town, Blists Hill. The local policeman is well liked and there is little trouble outside the New Inn public house (**15**) at closing time. All employers want sober staff which means the temperance movement has some influential followers in the town. The British Workmen refreshment room on the Wharfage in Ironbridge is an example of their zeal in trying to persuade people away from the evils of drink.

The community is typically God fearing as well. Everyone is either 'church' or 'chapel' with the Methodists attracting perhaps the

largest congregations. Throughout the 19th century there have been numerous special rallies and open air meetings, 'revivals' as they are called, with first the Church of England and then the Methodists encouraging the locals to become Christians (**38**). The building of the little 'tin chapel' (**54**) as it is affectionately called by the Church of England, in the 1880s just outside the main town was to give the iron workers, miners and their families somewhere to worship in that remote area. That, of course, was when the Hay Inclined Plane (**56**) was still working, taking tub boats loaded with coal from the top of the canal at Blists Hill down to the riverside at Coalport. Once a wonder of the age when completed in 1793, it's another thing that's closed down in the last few years.

Religion and the promise of a better life after death with no hardship or pain have certainly proved a comfort for the old. Not that this is all religion has to offer, but becoming too old and frail to earn a living is probably working class people's worst nightmare especially if they don't have a family to support them. Ending your days in the workhouse is still feared by many. You try and work as long as you can. There's no retirement age and no old age pension yet, though Parliament have been debating it. Some reckon it won't happen until 1909.

Nevertheless, Blists Hill people do know how to enjoy themselves. When the fair pitches up next to the ironworks there's much fun to be had on the rides and swings (**43**). Any excuse and the community will organise a good bonfire, and the fireworks and decorations used to celebrate HM Queen Victoria's Diamond Jubilee in 1897 were a sight to be seen.

It is amazing that working people can find so much time to do things other than work, with all sorts of hobbies and pursuits being enjoyed by the locals (**16**). Physical fitness amongst Blists Hill's young men was given a boost by the exploits of Captain Matthew Webb from nearby Dawley when he became the first man to swim the English Channel in 1875. Recently, the vicar of Madeley has complained that the passion for amusement, especially football, has made his job more difficult. That town's football club was established in 1885 and it also boasts a cricket club as well. The craze for bicycling (**3**) amongst the middle classes (even women)

is certainly catching on in the area with the nearby Forest Glen Refreshment Pavilion (**45**) patronised by members of the Cyclists' Touring Club, a national organisation founded in 1878.

Of course, it's not only physical recreation that appeals to Blists Hill folk. The doctor and those of his class are quite prepared to travel by train to Birmingham to hear performances of Mendelssohn's oratorio 'Elijah' at the Town Hall, for example, whilst others content themselves with concerts given by the Ironbridge Orchestra and Choir. Quite a number of ordinary working people have good singing voices and play musical instruments. There are hopes of forming a brass or silver band like the successful one over the river in Jackfield.

Who knows what might happen in the future. Only a few years ago it took weeks for letters to be exchanged between friends and family who had emigrated to Australia or Canada; now it's easy to stay in touch by going to the Canal Street Post Office (**9**) and by sending a message over the telegraph. They say it won't be long before Blists Hill gets its first telephone line. And whilst thinking about the Post Office and communications, who would have thought those early 'Penny Black' postage stamps of 1840 would become collectors' items? There's even a shop that opened a few years ago down in London trading under the name 'Stanley Gibbons', that specialises in selling old stamps from all over the world. Whatever next!

All aspects of life seem to have changed since Queen Victoria first came to the throne in 1837. Some believe the changes are improvements; others are not so sure. Older Blists Hill residents still think gas lights, with those uncanny mantles that never catch fire, are far too bright. There is talk of lighting houses with electricity but currently that can only happen if you have your own generator. The nearest electricity generating power station is in Wolverhampton, opened recently in 1895. Some even believe that electricity will take over from steam engines in industry and that in the future people will use it to heat their homes, shops and offices instead of coal fires. Perhaps those same clever people believe that one day we'll all be travelling in electric trains and even be flying!

ABOVE: watercolour by Warrington Smyth of Blists Hill furnaces, 1847
LEFT: Blists Hill Ironworks under construction in the 1980s
BOTTOM: Blists Hill furnaces, c.1900
RIGHT: the blowing engines – David & Sampson – being extracted from the Priorslee Works of the Lilleshall Company, St Georges, Telford, 1971

BLISTS HILL
History in the Making

The creation of Blists Hill Victorian Town started back in 1967. At the time, Britain was changing rapidly. Old buildings all over the country were being knocked down, tower blocks were going up, and heavy industry was in decline. Traditional crafts were disappearing and there was a real sense that the country was losing its industrial heritage.

However, in Shropshire something exciting was happening. At exactly the moment a new town – Telford – was being laid out on the exhausted industrial landscape of the East Shropshire Coalfield, the Ironbridge Gorge Museum Trust was created. Its aim was to preserve artefacts and significant industrial sites in what is now the Ironbridge World Heritage Site. Social history objects, Coalport China, decorative tiles and many more historic items were collected for display in a number of planned new museums. But something more than a museum was the intention for Blists Hill where a derelict 20 hectare site had been acquired. It was to be an open-air, industrial park where industrial processes and craft skills could be demonstrated to the public. Existing monuments on the site – a section of the Shropshire Canal, the Hay Inclined Plane (**56**), the Madeley Wood blast furnaces (**41**) and that firm's brick and tile works (**31**) – were also to be brought back to life. Nothing on this scale had been attempted before in this country.

Volunteers and a support organisation called the Friends of the Ironbridge Gorge Museum were vital in these early years (as they still are today), rescuing exhibits both large and small, organising fund-raising events and acting as guides. By 1977, two huge blowing engines (**47**) had been installed on site, part of the canal was reopened and tracks put back on the Inclined Plane. The most impressive achievement of this early period of the new open-air museum's life took much longer to complete. In a vast early 19th-century shed removed from Woolwich Arsenal, with equipment salvaged from a works in Bolton, a wrought ironworks was brought back to life (**40**). After a decade in the making it was commissioned by HRH The Prince of Wales in 1987, producing wrought iron again for the first time in a generation.

But by then the focus of Blists Hill had shifted as people and not processes became the new priority. Efforts turned to recreating a coherent environment in which visitors could experience what it was like to live and work when Britain was the Workshop of the World at the very end of the 19th century. Blists Hill Open Air Museum became Blists Hill Victorian Town.

At first buildings due for demolition were rescued and reconstructed on site by museum craftsmen (**53**). Probably the best examples of their brick by brick work are the Candle Factory (**33**) and Stirchley school (**46**). One of the most challenging projects was the dismantling and re-erection of a local timber-framed building that now houses the Estate Office (**37**). If whole buildings could not be saved, original fittings such as windows, doors and complete interiors were collected and incorporated into new structures; the New Inn (**15**), the Chemist's Shop/Pharmacy (**5**) and the Locksmith's (**28**) are all examples of this approach. In the case of Lloyd's Bank (**2**), a faithful replica of the existing bank at Broseley was created.

For over a decade the museum managed to open a new exhibit every year, and this was not just buildings. Between 1983 and 1992, the rotting remains of a Lower Severn Trow – The Spry –

ABOVE: HRH The Prince of Wales and Keith Gale a leading expert on the British Iron Industry, at the opening of the Ironworks, 6th March 1987

ABOVE: Stafford Place, St Georges, Telford, c.1905 which was copied in 2008 for the facade of no.3 Canal Street

MAIN PICTURE: demolition of the brick drying sheds' chimney in the 1960s where no.1 Canal Street now stands

LEFT: part of the original box-frame of 15/15a Holly Road, Little Dawley, Telford being re-erected as the Estate Office, spring 1990
BELOW: Shelton Toll House under construction, spring 1973
BOTTOM LEFT: some of Stirchley School's numbered bricks, 1992
BOTTOM RIGHT: The Spry on her way from Gloucester to Blists Hill, 27th March 1983

were transformed on site into a fully operational vessel (**48**). Originally launched in 1894, it was relaunched 98 years later in 1996, remaining under sail until returned to Blists Hill in 1997. Another pioneering project was the building of a replica of the world's very first steam locomotive constructed in Coalbrookdale in the winter of 1802/3 to the designs of Richard Trevithick. The replica was built by apprentices at GKN Sankey in Telford at the end of the 1980s and after running for a while in Coalbrookdale, it found a permanent home on Blists Hill (**30**).

During the 1990s there was a period of consolidation on site and then in 2009, in one major construction project, six new 'old' buildings along with a new visitor centre (**1**), mine railway and experience (**51**) and inclined lift (**50**) were completed. All this was achieved by employing a commercial building contractor working with a civil engineering company.

As well as augmenting the range of typical small trades and services in the main town area (**7–13**), it was an opportunity to add domestic housing to the site that had been missing from Blists Hill for too long (**10–13**). A decision was also made to erect buildings of different periods using a variety of new heritage bricks to emphasise those period differences. From a nondescript lane, Canal Street was transformed into a busy Victorian thoroughfare. Every building except the Post Office (**9**) was a copy of an existing structure in the East Shropshire Coalfield area. The museum's extensive collection of historic photographs and images from other organisations were used to get the details right. Great care was taken to make the whole street look as though it was a snap-shot from the past brought back to life. As many old fittings as possible were used from the Museum's collections and paint colours were chosen from a 1901 trade catalogue that actually included a colour chart that was in colour!

But Blists Hill has never been just a museum of buildings and old things. When the decision was made in the 1980s to put museum staff into Victorian costume, carefully replicated from original patterns, a new standard of interpretation was born. The site came to life. Since then, professional actors have added another dimension to street life, and special themed events have helped emphasise the significance of customs and traditions in the lives of ordinary working class Victorians.

Over the years many people and organisations have helped make Blists Hill what it is today. Financial and professional support has come from many sources too numerous to list here. There has been much help in kind as well as a lot of hard physical labour from both young and old. What they have all had in common, however, has been enthusiasm, and ultimately, that has been the most important element in the shaping of Blists Hill Victorian Town.

Where Next?

Why not explore our other attractions in the
Ironbridge Gorge World Heritage Site?

Museum of Iron

Coalport China Museum

Jackfield Tile Museum

Enginuity

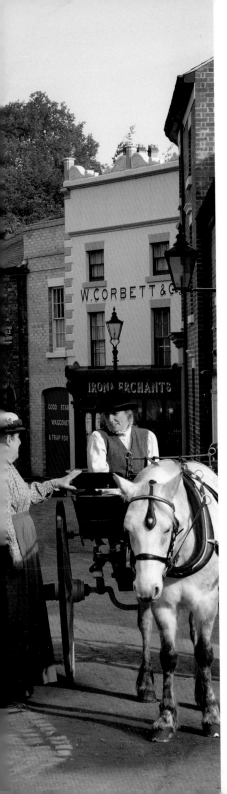

BLISTS HILL

Plan

1	Visitor Centre
2	Lloyd's Bank
3	Cycle Showroom
4	Grocer
5	Chemist
6	Goods Shed
7	Iron Merchants
8	General Draper and Outfitters
9	Post Office and Stationers and Museum of the Post Office in the Community
10	Photographer
11	Sweet Shop
12	Wash House
13	Fried Fish and Chipped Potato Shop
14	Cobbler's Shop
15	New Inn Public House (Restaurant and Toilets)
16	Boys' Brigade Hut
17	Butcher
18	The Iron Foundry
19	Jesse's Fold
20	Printer and Stationer's Shop
21	Plumber
22	Decorative Plasterer
23	Tinsmith
24	Machine Shop
25	Mason's Yard
26	Lee Dingle Plateway Bridge
27	Pleasure Gardens
28	Locksmith
29	Winding Engine
30	The Trevithick (seasonal)
31	Brick and Tile Works
32	Mine
33	Candle Factory
34	Sawmill & Undertaker
35	Harness Maker
36	Bakery (Bread products sold here)
37	Estate Office
38	Gospel Car
39	Doctor's Surgery
40	G.R. Morton Ironworks
41	Blast Furnaces
42	Ironworks Offices
43	Victorian Fairground (seasonal)
44	Blacksmith
45	Forest Glen Refreshment Pavilion (Café and Toilets)
46	Stirchley Board School
47	Blowing Engines
48	The Spry
49	The Green
50	Inclined Lift
51	Mine Railway and Mine Experience
52	Squatter's Cottage
53	Shelton Toll House
54	Mission Church
55	Miner's Walk
56	The Hay Inclined Plane

Food outlets

1, 13, 15, 17, 36 and 45 all serve food at various times.
Numbers 1 and 45 offer café and restaurant facilities respectively.

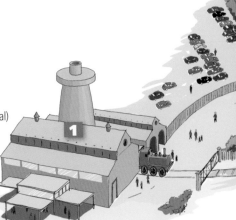